A Comedian's
Prayer Book

A Comedian
Travel Desk

HODDER
STOUGHTON

A Comedian's Prayer Book

Frank Skinner

**HODDER &
STOUGHTON**

First published in Great Britain in 2021 by Hodder & Stoughton
An Hachette UK company

4

Copyright © Frank Skinner, 2021

A CIP catalogue record for this title is available from the British Library

Hardback ISBN 978 1 529 36895 6
eBook ISBN 978 1 529 36897 0

Typeset in Adobe Caslon by Manipal Technologies Limited

Printed and bound in Great Britain by Clays Ltd, Elcograf S.p.A.

Hodder & Stoughton policy is to use papers that are natural, renewable
and recyclable products and made from wood grown in sustainable
forests. The logging and manufacturing processes are expected to
conform to the environmental regulations of the country of origin.

Hodder & Stoughton Ltd
Carmelite House
50 Victoria Embankment
London EC4Y 0DZ

www.hodderfaith.com

For Buzz,

Who trails more 'clouds of glory' than anyone I know.

INTRODUCTION

A COMEDIAN'S PRAYER BOOK. The title is a worry, isn't it? Is it a comedy book that merely uses prayer as a vehicle for its gags? No. The writer of such a book runs the risk of finding himself exiled to that most desolate of all places: the Humour Section. Is it, then, a prayer book specifically for comedians? No. I've been a professional comedian for over thirty years and, during that time, the religious believers I've met among my fellow japesters would, if assembled, just about fill a Vauxhall Corsa. Why go to the trouble of writing a whole book when a simple group-email would suffice?

Gather round for the metaphor. Imagine someone on a pilgrimage, stopping at churches, martyr-related tourist spots and sacred wells, while dressed in a medieval jester outfit. The intention is serious and completely devout, but the pilgrim just feels more at home in the motley than in sackcloth and ashes. He feels jest is an integral part of who he is and it seems wrong to deny that part. His whole life – his experiences, thoughts, opinions, beliefs – has been, he believes, defined and enriched by the accompaniment of the jesterial bells. Non-pilgrims – wry observers who just happen to find themselves adjacent to the sacred route – feel betrayed that the seeming satire of the motley is, it turns out, undermined by the clear evidence of internal belief. His fellow pilgrims, meanwhile, are outraged that his surface appearance does not reflect his inner conviction. They conclude that his belief must be faulty. For them it's church bells or no bells at all. He feels that both sets of bells can co-exist, indeed MUST co-exist; that the summoning toll from the high tower needs some light jingling as a humanising counterpoint. He even dares to venture that such jingling might act as a guard against the faithful becoming the fundamentalist, the compassionate becoming the unyielding and the atheist becoming the hater. Metaphor over.

So what are these prayers? Not verbatim transcriptions of my own prayers. You can't give a word-for-word account of something that has no words. Prayer, for me at least, is a telepathic dip into a long, ongoing conversation with thousands of tabs left open and no helpful 'new readers start here' summaries or simplifications for the neutral observer. If I tried to present these prayers in anything like their original form, it would be, for you, like reading a text message sent between two intimates, devoid of context, devoid of tone or motivation, devoid of the normal spelling, punctuation or vocabulary, and devoid of any clear response from the receiver, assuming, and I do, that there is one. Those of you who have read James Joyce's *Finnegans Wake* would probably have a ready-to-go coping strategy, but others would just be confused and upset. No. To use theatrical terminology, I've tried to retain the bare candour of the simple rehearsal-room improvisation, but infused it with all the production values required to make it a passable public entertainment. I've taken my convictions, my questions, my fears, my doubts, my elations, and presented them in what I think is an eavesdropper-friendly form. Hell, judgement, atheism, money, faith and the X-Men all feature.

It's a bit like reading the Bible, except you only get one side of the conversation and all the jokes are left in.

Is there a place for comedy in prayer? If there's a place for comedy in life, there's a place for comedy in prayer. God is a tough audience as far as audible response is concerned, but I love that I don't have to explain the references.

I am a practising Roman Catholic, so, inevitably, the book is a bit on the Catholic side in its understandings and imagery, though I doubt it would get a papal imprimatur. In truth, even other Christians can find us Catholics a bit exotic. I understand that. They lack our continental taste for statue-kissing, entrail-centric saint-depictions and skeletons in bridal veils. Those are the bits I love best. I looked up the word 'believer' on Thesaurus.com and the offered synonyms were adherent, devotee, disciple, follower, supporter, zealot, convert and freak. I like to think I cover all those bases in this book.

Of course, believers are also notoriously po-faced, as indeed are atheists, so I may have come up with a formula that alienates and annoys just about everyone. Anyway, I've written a prayer book. At least no one can accuse me of being too commercial.

GOD. I GUESS you know what I'm going to say in this prayer. And what I'll say in the next prayer. You know everything I'll ever pray, including this actual sentence. You also, of course, know what my final prayer will be. Chances are, even I won't know it's my final prayer. I'll just pray as usual, my mind wandering between the divine and the domestic. That person crying on the bus, breakfast, Jacob wrestling the angel, wooden floor against knees. I won't know it's my swansong. Pity. I'd have liked a sort of final summing-up, like an after-dinner speaker. 'It's been a heaven of a journey' – that sort of thing. But I'll just mutter my way through with no sense of specialness. I can't see a way round that. I don't think a *carpe diem* approach would be appropriate. (I like to throw in a bit of Latin, every now and then, just for you.) I can't pray every prayer as if it's my last. I'm all for being impassioned, but not on a daily basis. Mortality-driven sincerity is exhausting. I want my prayers to be dynamic but not actually cardiovascular. There has to be light and shade.

Anyway, as I said, you know how this one will go. I won't waste your time with a spoiler alert. 'Your Father knoweth what things ye need before you ask for them' or something like that. So why do I ask for anything? Why do I pray at all? I once read an interview with Johnny Cash, talking about his good friend, Bob Dylan. Cash said he and Dylan were so close they would sometimes fish, side by side, for four or five hours without speaking. (So that's Latin and now a fish-based anecdote. You see how I tailor these prayers specifically for you.) I'd like to think you and I are at least as close as Johnny Cash and Bob Dylan. I can't tell you anything about me you don't already know. In fact, I'm the one who needs the feedback. You should be doing the talking. Of course, your voice would be so mighty, like a wind on a mountain, that I'd just get a migraine. I think the answer might be in that Bob-and-Johnny silence.

When I pray, words do sometimes seem a bit cumbersome, even inappropriate. There's a silent, nearly non-breathing place I occasionally stumble across that feels like it might be close to where you are. Not the same postcode, but, I think, adjacent. And all the hard work of prayer – coming up with neat phrases, innovative requests, jokes even, generally trying not to bore you: yes, I do worry about boring you – seems to melt away. As I said, I'm aware that you know what I'm going to say next, but I still feel I owe it to you to say it as elegantly as possible. I don't want to be like that slothful servant who buried his talent in the ground, thus offering his returning master no increase. You gave me the words; I'm trying to make the most of them.

I imagine you flicking through Heaven's super-multiple prayer-channels, listening to all our pleading and praise: 'my poor wife'; 'if I could just pass this exam'; 'hallowed be thy name'; 'I'm so afraid'. Flicking, flicking, trying to find something that earns more than just a tick for effort or a cross in the 'be careful what you pray for' box. I know we're told to keep knocking at the door, but I'm worried that if the knocking continues in the same dull rhythm, you'll eventually opt for earplugs. Anyway, all that hard work of prayer is sometimes, not every day, replaced by a yearning to just be. To silently be. It isn't not-praying. It feels more like being prayed.

I never hear your voice – no mighty wind – or, if I do, I don't recognise it, but I have sensed you in the silence. And I rest there for just a short time. I sort of know it's where the glory is, but it's a place I feel too naked to stay long. I also feel, and I don't mean to reduce you, that the silence might be the one place that you don't know what's coming next, either.

You SEEM A long way away tonight. Maybe it's me.
Maybe I don't want you to hear me too clearly.

OH, MIGHTY, OMNIPOTENT, omniscient, tremendously brilliant God. I, who am worth slightly less than the smeared remains of a gnat on a windscreen, give you praise. Yes, I give you praise. In that sense, I suppose, I'm a traditionalist. Sort of. The truth is I really don't imagine you're sitting in Paradise thinking, 'You know, what I *really* need is a bit more praise.' But I could be wrong about that. Maybe praise is something you actually do need. Maybe that's what we got created for. I know the angels have sung your praise since the old days, but maybe humankind is a supplementary praise-supply unit. If so, I fear our group output is fading fast. If angel-praise is the treble to our bass, the overall sound must seem quite tinny at this moment in history.

I'm not suggesting, of course, that you're some sort of praise-junkie. I just mean that the praise, to you, might feel like a caress. A cathedral choir or a hallelujah chorus might seem like a full-blown ticker-tape parade when it leaves us, in our near-insignificant smallness, but by the time it reaches the vast expanses of you, it probably feels like an index finger gently brushing your cheek.

That's what worries me. My individual prayer-praise is, at best, economical, downplayed even. I don't have a problem with the subservience. I'm happy on my knees, happy on my belly. The New Testament redefined humility as a power-source. My palms, together in prayer, sometimes seem to crackle with energy. I realise it could just be the nylon carpet. To lie prostrate before you has become the believer's badge of honour. Such reduction of self seems the antithesis of modernity. It challenges the fundamental concept of the twenty-first century: the cult of the significant individual. The aim, instead, is to un-me oneself. Like the great medieval artists whose work remained unsigned. Then again, to celebrate my dazzling capacity to be truly humble is, of course, somewhat contradictory.

My problem is that it's so hard to come up with praise for you that feels, well, fresh. There's scarcely any room at the top end of praise: the 'almighty', 'all-powerful', 'I'm just insect-remains and you're magnificent' end. For me, the way forward is the understated, bittersweet end of praise. That seems to fit me better. Although, as we've established, it's not about me. I do completely acknowledge your all-powerfulness. It's just that it's not on my 'Top Three Favourite Qualities of God' list. Off the top of my head, those qualities would be: 1. Loving, 2. Interesting and 3. Defiantly uncool. Admittedly, it's a subjective list and it changes on a regular basis. I'll keep you posted.

Anyway, if I work my way past the rhetoric, past the Deity-pleasing, and dig deep, my instinctive praise-mode would be along the lines of 'I'm always glad when I've remembered to turn to you'. It's not especially catchy, but when I say it, things go quiet. I go quiet. Your strength and my weakness are implicit, but not hammered home.

I could say, 'You are the stillness at the core of me.' It is true, but I acknowledge it does sound a little bit yoga-ish and I'm never sure how you feel about the Eastern religions. I like to think it's the same you at the centre of every religion, just viewed from a different angle, but, suddenly, I'm remembering the golden calf incident and deciding to move on. Nevertheless, before I do, I must say I think yoga has many benefits, and I think it's a shame that you've allowed the Eastern deities to have something of a monopoly on religious practice with a strong physical fitness element. I certainly think Christianity could be classified, without any loss of gravitas, as part of the wellness industry, and that it's a real pity that we're not, for whatever reason, exploiting that particular mailing list. Of course, if, as I suspect, you *are* the Eastern deities, there's no more to be said.

Anyway, that's enough marketing advice. Back to the praise. What about, 'You fill me with peace'? I have to stop this now. I'm actually asking you to pick your own adulation. Worship was never meant to be multiple choice.

What I'm trying to do here, I realise, is to stay humble, to switch off my status-light, while still championing my self-penned, sparklingly original praise-style. A lot of the ticker-tape seems to be blowing back in my direction.

Oh, universe-moulding, life-or-death-deciding, totally top-drawer almightyness, make me truly humble, but humble in a really fascinating way.

Jesus. You say in Luke's Gospel that when we do charitable works, we should do them in secret, not sounding a trumpet about our generosity so that we might reap 'the glory of men'. God will know and that should be enough. This advice makes complete sense, but it has, nevertheless, almost certainly cost me an MBE.

I HAD A charity request arrive in the post, today. It was a good cause – helping people with some illness or other – but the letter began 'Dear Stephen'. I know these requests are sent to a lot of people, but I do believe that if you're asking someone to help you, you should at least get their name right. Then it occurred to me that I'm in the habit of addressing you as 'God', as, for example, in everyday requests like, 'Please, God, help me to be less impatient with the incompetent loafers who surround me.' I suddenly got quite anxious about this. I hadn't really thought about it before, but it's possible, of course, that getting the name right could be absolutely crucial. All the good things I've done in my life – it would be crass of me to offer examples – could be rendered void because, in my discourse with you, I accidentally adopted the wrong form of address. I'm perfectly aware of my failings. Well, not 'perfectly', obviously. *You're* perfectly aware of my failings. I only have an unreliable general sense of them. But enough to know it's not completely out of the question that I might end up on Satan's griddle. I say it's not completely out of the question, but that might just be me being tactical. I don't know if you're aware of this – I'm guessing that's something people don't often say to you – but there is a temptation to be a bit tactical when praying. I mean, you hold all the cards and it's scary that one might say the wrong thing and create an indelible black mark. So when I say I might end up on Satan's griddle, I'm not being totally sincere. The truth is that when the Great Segregation comes and good and evil are placed in their respective ghettoes, I feel I'd slot in better with the former group. Whenever I see evil types, on the news or in some disturbing documentary, I always think how unlike me they are. We wouldn't have two words to say to each other. I know the afterlife is not all about meeting people, but inevitably there'll be a community of sorts, and if I end up in Evil-town I just don't think

I'll have much to contribute. So when I suggest I might end up as a guest of the Dark Destroyer (actually I think that was the boxer, Nigel Benn's nickname) I'm being a bit disingenuous. Though I say it as shouldn't, I think posting me to Hell would be really harsh. As for Goodtown, I'm not saying I should be your first phone call, but I really think it's a place that would bring out the best in me. The danger is, of course, that in saying this, I could be provoking your limitless fury. 'I'll be the judge of that', you might say, and if you ever think of adopting a catchphrase you could do a lot worse.

SOMETIMES, WHEN I kneel here like this, I can smell my first confession: fear and wonder.

SINCE WE LAST spoke – well, since I last spoke – I've been thinking about Hell. I'll be straight with you: it's unsettled me somewhat and, well, there are a few things I'd like to try and clarify. I do realise, given that you pride yourself on your 'mysterious ways', that I probably shouldn't be probing you about admin. Then again, I think the poet and clergyman George Herbert said something like 'Why give dust a tongue and then not listen to it speak?' Ironically, this whole thing came about because I was imagining myself in Heaven. I'll give you the basic scenario. I've just arrived in Paradise and, after a few hours of celebratory handshaking and yet another mouthful of leaves from a nearby chocolate tree (Heaven, for me, has never completely distinguished itself from the Big Rock Candy Mountain), I say to a smiling official, 'I'd really like to see my mum now', and he replies, 'Have you tried the Scotch Egg Plant?' and I get a sudden knotted feeling in my stomach and say, with a little more edge, 'No, I'd really like to see my mum now, please'. I see him pick a barely noticeable blossom petal from a mother-of-pearl colonnade and examine it between his fingers. 'Frank,' he says, surprisingly opting for my stage-name, 'your mum didn't make it.' That moment. How do such officials react when one of the saved is so shaken, he is physically sick? And it's on my robe and on the weird white AstroTurf flooring. Eventually, I wipe the chocolatey slime from my mouth and ask, calmly, 'Is she in Hell?' and he just looks down at the dry ice and sighs. What do I do then, knowing my mum, who always held my hand when I crossed the road, is suffering eternal torture and humiliation? Do I shrug, meaningfully, and then scamper over to those giggling blonde girls playing frisbee? Actually, where are all the brunettes? I'll ask later. I receive and deliver the spinning disc amid flash-frames of my mother, her naked, wrinkled body pierced by grinning demons. And I'm supposed to stick with that Jesus Army smile and never question the masterplan. I know I'll struggle with that. We're built to love and then you broil the subject of that love because she spent the money that was supposed to pay Auntie Lynne's electricity bill on food for me and my siblings. I wonder if Auntie Lynne made it to Paradise. I guess she'd already served her time in darkness. Either way, if you asked her about my mum, I bet she wouldn't want to press charges. She was the forgiving type. Yes, my mother probably committed other, less-justifiable, sins, and I know I've chosen the hungry children motif for extra emotional impact, but we're talking about horned demons and eternal flames, so don't make me out to be the melodramatic one.

I am promised eternal bliss if I'm a good person, but such bliss, knowing that my mother, or anyone else for that matter, smoulders and screams, can only be achieved by an unimaginable amount of callous indifference. Is that what the saved become? Are they raised above human traits like compassion and empathy? I expect supra-tropical temperatures in the pit, but it now occurs to me that Heaven might be icy cold, with inmates to match. How else could one cope with that distant screaming?

My admittedly unreliable instinct tells me that anyone who can turn a deaf ear to the desperate pleadings of the condemned shouldn't have a place in your new world. But I guess you knew what you were looking for when you interviewed them. If there is a Hell and it is a smoke-filled cave of cruelty, I might feel more at home among the blistering sinners than the cold-hearted competition winners.

I always liked that Jesus hung out with sinners. It made me feel potentially understood. I suppose I imagined his behaviour was habitual. If so, I see Jesus, now a shady underground figure, teardrop-lines on soot-covered cheeks, appearing from behind a glowing rock to ease the thirst of the half-submerged, with wine turned into water. Heavenly officials attending yet another 'Thank God we made it' parade, looking at their watches. 'Where is Jesus? Who's going to do the medals?' But Jesus isn't there. He's down among the unforgivable. Too late for missionary work. Too late even for healing. Just soothing now. A few gulps, a mopped brow, a poisoned barb deftly removed. Still with the sinners after all these years. Meanwhile, in my cowardice, I reach for the frisbee. The blonde girls shriek. My mother takes her two-hundredth punch to the face and I, in my Glory, try not to think about it.

She had her chance. She said no when she could have said yes, or yes when she could have said no. They all did. Let them burn. That'll be me in Heaven. No one likes a trouble-maker. That's how you get crucified.

YOU SEEM VERY far away, tonight. My prayers are trapped in my head, caught up in the whirl of earthliness. I suppose praying is like parking: you get as close as you can.

I WANTED TO talk some more about the God-thing, about referring to you as 'God' when we have these chats. My main concern, in this respect (I'm not enjoying this sentence so far. I hate it when my prayers start to sound like a letter to the council) is to do with the whole Holy Trinity thing. I'm very confused. I'm guessing God is a sort of umbrella term, incorporating all three of you. The way I see it, it's as if one wrote a letter to the popular mutant superhero ensemble, the X-Men. It would be, I think, acceptable to begin such a letter 'Dear X-Men', figuring that whichever X-Man (I'm not totally sure the singular form is acceptable) opened the letter, they would take it upon themselves to write the reply. I realise the X-Men are probably not the best analogy because, of course, they don't exist, but you'll take my general point about team responsibility.

Anyway, my problem is I never know if I'm speaking to the Father, the Son or the Holy Spirit. Or indeed some combination of these, up there in Heaven, on a sort of conference call. I know 'up there' is a vague concept, but I'm an old-fashioned believer, in many ways, and I still think of Heaven as the next floor after outer space or, as you probably call it, inner space. I definitely feel that the Father and the Son are up there. I'm basing this on two main pieces of evidence: you, Father, are often portrayed as a booming voice from above, and you, Jesus, were last seen heading in a skyward direction. I've always felt that you, Holy Spirit, were left down here to fill the gap left by Jesus, a sort of roving ambassador from Heaven.

Let's return to that letter-to-the-X-Men analogy. Imagine such a letter was opened by, say, Wolverine (a man seemingly designed for letter-opening). Given that the letter begins 'Dear X-Men', he would probably end up reading it aloud to the assembled group, in their communal chill-area. Then each mutant would take from it whatever moved or interested them. Now I'll be honest with you, I'm not really sure of the demarcation as far as the Holy Trinity is concerned. Do you each have your specialist topics? I suppose you, Jesus, are the obvious entrance point for the praying Earthling because you're the only one of the Trinity to have experienced actual flesh-time. That seems to make you a bit more graspable. My eight-year-old son, as you know, speaks exclusively to you. 'Good morning to Jesus. I give you this day, all that I think and do and say ...' or 'Goodnight to Jesus. I come to say, thank you for your love today ...' (I should try a rhyming prayer some time. Can you imagine? Well, obviously, you can.) Then again, when you, during your Earth-sojourn, were asked how we should pray, you addressed your example-prayer to the Father. That suggests we should indeed pray to the Father, but, as I mentioned, you were on Earth at the time so you couldn't really tell people to pray to you. That would be like phoning someone in the same room.

There is a further issue here. Forgive me if this is a bad thing to say, but I feel God the Father is probably the least approachable of the Trinity. That thought makes me sad. As a Father, myself, admittedly on a smaller scale, the one thing I always strive to maintain is approachability. I want to offer an embrace, not that delicate touching of fingernails we see on the Sistine Chapel ceiling. The plagues, the fireballs, the pillars of salt – they do suggest a certain strictness.

If it's Jesus who's opened this particular prayer-letter, maybe it's better if you don't read that last paragraph out loud. Then again, I don't feel right asking you to keep secrets from each other. Actually, there's probably a telepathic thing that makes that impossible.

As for praying to you, Holy Spirit, my main problem is that I tend to think of you as, well, smoke. Magical, enigmatic, inspirational, nurturing smoke, but smoke, nonetheless. I think this is because you appeared to the disciples as flame. I don't imagine my experience of you can ever be that dynamic, but, as with a candle, when the flame goes out and is replaced by smoke, the remaining odour becomes stronger, richer, more pervasive. I feel you, Holy Spirit, are already within me, already inhaled, there at the source of my fears and joys and questioning. I feel you are my prayer-mate. Perhaps still a flame after all, but one that flickers at the heart of me, enabling my communion with the other two, with their combined roles, love and boundaries. I'll just say the words and you'll be my transmitter, and, I feel it now, my receiver, my link to the unfathomable centre.

I didn't really know I thought all that until I just said it out loud. My initial exhilaration is soon tempered by sorrow. I am such an inadequate dwelling place.

I JUST WANTED to ask: what is better, to reach out or to reach in?

So, THIS RICH man, camel, eye-of-a-needle thing. I'm assuming it's an impenetrable metaphor, its meaning lost in the thick curtain-folds of time. Jesus, you would struggle, in this instance, to defend yourself against accusations of rich-ism. The well-heeled are always an easy target. I believe, as instructed, that we should do unto others as we would wish them to do unto us. Well, I hardly ever criticise the poor, not for being poor, anyway. It's about fairness. It seems the poor are Fosbury-Flopping through the eye of a needle without touching the sides. We should cry for the ultimately suffering rich. They are served their dessert first, the sugary sweetness masking the horrific main course to come. This life, after all, is no more than a brief and ramshackle rehearsal for eternity. The poor cruise through to shining glory, propelled by their sadness and suffering. The rich, however, are enjoying the equivalent of a pre-firing-squad cigarette, before the gun-smoke rises on their eternally painful execution.

Yes, I have a few bob in my pocket, so I've scrutinised this much-quoted passage at length. Imagine if there's one word missing from the Gospel text, an exhausted scribe rendering an understandable error. What if it should, it turns out, have said, 'It's easier for a camel eyelash to pass through the eye of a needle than for a rich man to get into Heaven'? At last, I could enjoy some of this money I've worked so hard for. Hard work that would have been pointless without some God-given talent at the core. Should I spell accomplice with a capital A? I could give my money to the poor, but then they wouldn't be poor any more and I'd be robbing them of their Fast Track to Paradise.

So, as I say, I'm guessing the whole camel-thing is a now-unfathomable example of some ancient symbolism. Or a typo. We should just accept that its truth is unknowable and move on.

Having said that, I heard a theory that there was one particular gate for entering Jerusalem, commonly known as the 'eye of the needle'. Only skinny, ascetic wild men from the desert and other low-carbs prophets could squeeze through. This, some claim, is the 'eye of the needle' in question. If so, I'm assuming you could probably, at a push, and I mean a push, get a camel through there. It would require a lot of determination and discipline, but so, I imagine, does salvation.

This gate story brings with it, it seems to me, a veiled suggestion that, when it comes to being saved, obesity might be a hindrance. Now I come to think about it, I've seen and enjoyed a lot of Christian art, but I can't recall ever seeing a fat Jesus. It just doesn't work. Early Christianity feels like a thin person's game. Hence 'enter by the narrow gate'. That would certainly explain why five loaves and two fishes was more than enough for the five thousand – 'Thanks, but I don't really do bread'. I wish the Bible gave a name to the first fat Christian. It must have been like when Heaven's entrance-conditions were broadened to include the Gentiles. Then again, chronic obesity, with its attendant illnesses, sound-tracked by the mocking cruelty of the ignorant, sounds like a 'Go straight to Heaven' card if ever there was one. Anyway, back to camels.

There is additional information suggesting that the 'eye of the needle' gate was not just narrow but also very low, so the camel would have to kneel to get through. Now we're getting the message: a lot of fasting and kneeling will speed your passage to the celestial hall. The camel-thing makes more sense in the light of this. The humps mean it absolutely has to kneel to get through. An ass, for example, another of what one might call 'the Bible animals', could probably just crouch a little. The last thing you want is a metaphor that suggests the afterlife can be accessed by stooping. To me, it sounds like the 'eye of the needle' gate (that actually sounds more like a scandal than a physical entrance) might be something that rich Christians commissioned builders to construct by way of a loophole. Like a crafty merchant who accidentally catches the Sermon on the Mount and then changes his name, by the ancient equivalent of deed poll, to The Meek, figuring it might prove profitable at a later date.

The other big get-out clause, of course, is the follow-up statement to the camel–needle shocker: the bit that goes: 'Of course, for God, everything is possible'. So, yes, *you* actually *could* get a camel through the eye of a needle, without resorting to an ancient gate technicality. It's a straightforward procedure for the omnipotent. Come to think of it, I once saw a street-performer squeeze his whole body through an unstrung tennis racquet. It's a start. State-of-the-art kitchen utensils could also provide the proverbial stairway to Heaven. One could liquidise a camel and then part the surface of the syrupy residue, Red-Sea-style, with a needle turned pointy-end upwards, possibly while shouting, 'Voila! There's still hope'. Of course, such impudence would probably make you furious – but also maybe just a little bit proud of your endlessly inventive creations.

Being rich certainly brings extra temptations, but these include the temptation to give money to the Church, to friends in need, to the poor, even to people in curly nylon wigs and unfashionable t-shirts, shaking plastic buckets – basically to spread the jam beyond one's own sandwich. When I was poor, my main temptations were theft, exploitation of others' kindness and non-declaration of earnings. Poverty didn't help my goodness, it helped justify my badness. Now I've got a few bob in my pocket, I have to try harder. Now there's a pile of coins on one end of my life-scales, I have to realign the balance by loading some practical compassion on the other. When I was poor, I had to concentrate on me because me was a full-time job. When I started earning, a lot of me didn't need worrying about any more, so I had scope to worry about someone else. Money, I think, has made me kinder. So, nowadays, when I hear the camel eye-of-a-needle thing, I fear for my post-death future, of course I do. But, interestingly, my first thought is not for myself. It's for that poor, forcibly compressed camel, its snout hard against the cold steel aperture, the victim of a desperate camel-owner who lacks my capacity for self-justifying nuance.

I DON'T KNOW that I've ever told you this, but I genuinely find the Bible to be a rattlingly good read. *Mazel tov.*

IT'S NOT COMPLICATED, is it, Christianity? It's just about being good. I know that sounds like a thing a child might say, but we're told in the Bible, if you don't mind me quoting it back to you, that being somehow like a little child is an important requisite of faith. I guess that means holding on to a purity of belief that's never arch, ironic or over-complicated by terms and conditions. Some crystal-clear oasis that still gently sparkles amid an otherwise grubbily mature mindset. I like holding on to that child-heart. William Wordsworth suggested we come into this material world still smelling of eternity, but gradually grow further and further away from that core of truth. But we must, it seems to me, keep a secret relic of our child-selves, still slightly glowing, wrapped in a cloth with a moon-and-stars motif; something of the source we can return to when we need replenishing.

So being good is just that. I don't have to relabel it with grown-up words and concepts. Yes, it is morality, and social conscience and compassion and piety, but they're all covered by 'being good'. Let's just be good.

There's an Elvis Presley song I love, a gospel song. It's called, 'I believe in the man in the sky'. That title seems bathed in child-glow. To describe you, in all your intricate and mysterious majesty, as 'the man in the sky' is so stark, so rampantly unsophisticated. It's like a deliberate statement of intent. The song's covert message seems to be, 'I'm not interested in a complicated theological analysis of words like "God" and "Heaven". I don't need context and calibration. Here's what I believe. I know it includes questionable use of both gender and geography, but that part of me that remains a child has no time for explanatory footnotes. The man in the sky is a good enough description of what I believe in. I make no apologies for its simplicity. Its simplicity is its strength.'

I, as you may have gleaned from our previous conversations, obsessively pore over your endless complications. I peer hopelessly through the dark smoke of the burning bush and all I do is make my eyes water. Sometimes, I need to just lie back in the warm bathwater of my child-faith, unflustered by niceties and nuance. Isn't all religious nuance a sort of apology to non-believers? We've apologised our way out of a ragged and reckless faith and into some bland approximation, a sort of belief-lite. The modern equivalent of bearing witness sounds something like, 'I don't believe in God, exactly, but I do feel there might be a sort of Universal Will that in some way generates a positive energy that, in a sense, informs our moral attitudes and what one might call spiritual instincts'. Oh, my God! And I mean that literally. I will not be joining the chorus of 'Oh, my Universal Will', commonly shortened, of course, to just OMUW!

I'm trying not to judge these apologisers. I know there's belief in there, somewhere. It just happens to be almost completely obscured by an 'I don't want people to think I'm strange' stencil. But there's still a tiny bit of child-glow seeping through the cracks. Still, my Father's house has many mansions. I'm guessing many varied expressions of faith find shelter there. My head may be befuddled by bush-smoke, but my heart's with the man in the sky. Without the child-faith, it's just words.

THEY SAY THE Devil has all the best tunes. But I bet he *hates* music. So even the having of all the best tunes is, for him, a punishment.

AM I KNEELING here because I believe in you or because I may need to believe in you at some future date? If terrible tragedy befalls me I may have only you to talk to. Turning to a stranger at such a time wouldn't seem right to me. So, and I'm speculating, I'm setting you up now, I'm building the shelter while the sun still shines, so that when storms come, I will not suddenly have to learn belief from scratch. I will have my history of rehearsed belief, an already-existing structure, an only lightly trodden staircase up which I can scamper to the level of full conviction. So that's what I'm asking: am I maintaining a receptacle – my prayer-life – into which I can pour my forged-in-desperation faith when the time arises? Is this kneeling, this prayer, an act of insurance?

What *do* I believe? I think that's the hardest question of all. I'm not sure I trust myself enough to answer it. I can accept, at least, the possibility that I'm investing in a faith that will kick in at some point in the future. I am able to think that little of myself. My faith, like that of most sane people, has ebbed and flowed: never left me, never set me aflame. I'm sure there are undulations to come. Not just for me but for every believer. I'm thinking, here, of the afterlife. Surely everyone's faith will change drastically at some point after death. It will either dissolve into silent nothingness or be replaced by the breathtakingly real. I expect even the faith of devout, unquestioning believers will be ramped up a few notches when they are actually in your presence. No one's faith could be of such certainty that, when you finally rear up before them, they will merely nod, mutter 'Ah, there you are' and then start quizzing you about the Immaculate Conception. Even the strongest faith is still only faith. On a league of belief-intensity, unchallengeable knowledge must rank higher than faith does.

But even as I say that, the words are bitter on my lips. I think I taste my own error. It's as if, in my internal world, the word 'faith' suddenly became illuminated, like somebody switched all its lights on. It is suddenly vivid against the darkness. Maybe, it now seems to me, faith is a more powerful thing than knowing. Faith isn't fuelled by the mundanities of fact. It seems to have a tangible existence of its own, broadcasting 24/7 on a higher wavelength that believers regularly tune into. It is a way of life rather than an opinion. It brings an intrinsic merit to the person of faith, a person who has moved beyond a cold reliance on proof. Faith is so recklessly counter-intuitive, so challenging, so dynamically un-modern, I'm getting excited just talking about it. I've noticed my prayer-hands are making a slight clapping motion.

But when, or if (he said, once again illustrating the incompleteness of his own faith), we are actually confronted by you – when believing is replaced by knowing – will that knowing be stronger than our earthly faith or might it be a lesser thing, diminished by the passivity of merely observing a fact?

If you ride across the sky into human history, flanked by dazzling angels, the whole world will believe, saint and sinner alike. Everyone will believe, but not everyone will have faith. Faith will be redundant. Faith, I realise, is a privilege, but a privilege with a sell-by date. I dance to the faith-music now, but it won't play for ever. It will be replaced by the louder, though I suspect more mainstream, music of manifested deity. I anticipate a change from minor to major. So, when finally confronted by your undeniable amazingness, we will gain absolute and universal certainty and lose all the multi-layered manifestations of individual faith.

Doubting Thomas, the only disciple who comes with his own adjective, seemed gutted to have the opportunity of faith taken away from him. We may get to prod the crucifixion wounds – oh, how the atheists will cower and crumble – but then, well, we don't get to be special any more. We just see and believe. No need for any input from us. Belief will cease to be interactive.

You know, the more I talk about faith the more I feel sure that I have it. Otherwise, why would I bemoan the prospect of losing it, even of losing it to certainty? I knelt, tonight, to present my lack of faith. I tried to think dangerously, to question my own motivations. I feel prayer is not the place to give yourself the benefit of the doubt. I'm here to confess, to offer myself up for inspection, to shine the light into my own dark corners. But, sometimes, you intervene. I honestly think you intervene. There's no voice, no sudden smell of incense. But somewhere in the swirl of me, you also become present. I spoke of doubt, but I'm not sure it was me who spoke of faith. I set out to undermine myself, but it feels now, as the prayer ends, like you just wouldn't let me. I feel a tear against my lash. I don't think it's cheek-bound. Just a bit of spontaneous welling. If it's crying at all it's certainly good crying. When it's bad crying you'll be the first to know.

THEY SAY THE Devil has all the best tunes. Maybe they just got confused by the term 'horn section'.

IS IT OKAY to pray for atheists? I've become self-conscious about it. I know they're a bit of a nightmare, but you're the past master of the left-field act of kindness. I saw an advert for a local gym. It offered members the chance to get free membership for a friend. I'm sure you don't want to be out-kinded by an organisation dedicated to specifically physical improvement. Of course, one complication is that my atheist friends (which means almost all of my friends) don't want to be prayed for. They'd be, at best, unimpressed if I told them. Especially if I told them exactly what I was praying for on their behalf. They would probably resent my use of phrases like 'come to their senses', 'finally see the light' and 'lost souls searching for Catholicism'. (Actually, you'll recognise that last phrase from my discussions with you about friends who *do* believe but are members of, what I like to call, the support religions. It's a surprisingly flexible phrase considering its core strength is its inflexibility.) I certainly didn't ask these Atheista for permission to pray for them. I'd rather hit them on their blind side. I think of it as a drive-by intercession.

You would be well within your rights – especially as your rights are limitless – to ask, in a world when you aren't, or so it seems, answering a lot of the faithful's pleadings, why you should waste your time – which, again, is limitless – on the smug, self-centred deniers that constitute so much of Western society, certainly in the UK. Especially as their requests must inevitably arrive via an intermediary. My response to this would be that these are good-ish people who are only a divine brain-implant away from a dramatic and possibly contagious conversion. You'd only need to set a few hundred of them aflame – and, yes, I mean spiritually – and soon droves of their fashion-following friends would start asking themselves the big questions. They won't want to be the last to convert, the last to acknowledge the changing mood, the last to recognise the new intellectual environment. They won't want to look like ambience chasers.

I'm not cutting a new groove here. As a kid, I remember praying, at my Catholic Junior School assembly, that Mary, Mother of Mercy, might 'enlighten the minds that are miserably enfolded in the darkness of ignorance and sin'. All I'm doing is putting names to this shadowy ensemble so the Blessed Virgin doesn't have to seek them amid the near-impenetrable atheist-gloom. It's the good-guy version of writing to the Stasi about your colleague's anti-government ramblings. There's nothing in this for me. Although it would be nice to get a bit more empathy during Lent. In truth, I'd be making things more difficult for myself, especially on the salvation front. If you came down to collect the deserving faithful this very afternoon, you'd find, I suspect, fairly slim pickings. Sorting out the saved will feel like a cosmic game of 'Where's Wally?' This grim scarcity is probably my best chance of mounting the cherry-picker to Paradise. If, however, at my beseeching, my atheist friends start having epiphanies like popcorn going off in a pan, the competition will get much tougher. Suddenly, I'd be trying to match myself against the zeal of the convert. Still, I'm hoping there must be some kind of advantage in booking the holiday early, as it were.

So, yes, I pray for the miserably enfolded. They are much more in need of your help than the believers, be they chronically sick or violently oppressed. These latter sufferings are very much of an earthly nature. Come the glorious day, their anguish will be left behind, like when those novelty items in an amusement arcade grab-a-gift machine are lifted from their cheerless chamber of materialism by a descending claw from above. The atheists, in contrast, have an illness that, if untreated, renders them sufferers for all eternity. Temporal torments of a physical nature are small beer compared to a significant endangering of the soul. This is Operation Lost Sheep. So shine the light of realisation on my atheist friends. Forgive their Richard-Dawkins-is-so-cool trend-following superficiality, their uninformed criticisms, their arrogant certainty, and let them see that, as it turned out, I was right all along.

THEY SAY THE Devil has all the best tunes. They should have heard me sing 'Soul of my Saviour', at St Hubert's School, when I was nine. Snotty and awkward but with the feeling of something pure flowing through me. How often does the Devil get a performance like that? I bet Aleister Crowley had a lousy singing-voice, with an embarrassing vibrato that he thought made him sound sinister.

I WAS THINKING about that dream. Or should I say *that* dream like they used to say *that* dress? I was clambering up the side of an enormous hole in the ground, the soil falling away beneath me. You (I knew it was you) stood at the lip of the hole, arms outstretched, looking like Abraham Lincoln: frock-coat, stovepipe hat, beard and – I still can't grasp the symbolism – noticeably bad teeth. And you said, in a gentle voice, 'I'm already here'. Do you remember? Are you party to our dreams as well as our waking thoughts? I'm actually blushing.

Anyway, *that* dream. It's the closest I've ever got to a bona fide religious experience and, let's be honest, it's not that close. It was only a dream, after all. If you'd actually appeared in my room and said, 'I'm already here', it would have been a very different experience. (Actually, given your Jewish connections, it might have made more sense if you'd said, 'I'm here, already'.) But the presence of you, the nearness – no offence, but even the thought of it is terrifying. There are moments, like that dream or the occasional mid-prayer tingle, that suggest echoes of true contact. Those moments seem to bring you nearer, make me less of-the-world, if only for the next hour or so. But the sharp proximity of an actual vision – I don't think I'd have the strength.

Take St Paul, thunderbolted and blind. To hear your gut-thumping voice of God and for that voice to be reproachful ... Of course, St Paul was made of stronger, sterner stuff. And yet what scares me most isn't the approaching fireball. It's the aftermath. It's the remaining responsibility of contact, of being singled out, of being mission-ised. Paul actually lost his life in your electrical storm. He lost his life and was presented with a replacement-life that you liked better. Yes, the scariest part of the Road to Damascus story isn't the lightning, the blinding or even your God-voice asking, 'Why do you persecute me?' These would be frightening, of course, but the bit that really makes me tremble is the calm certainty of your words, 'Now get up and go into the city, and you will be told what you must do' – the sudden withdrawal of the Free Will agreement, replaced by the tyranny of 'must'. It's hard to tell you all this, partly because I know you'll be angered by my lack of commitment to the cause and partly because I might be setting myself up for an apposite response. I'm looking at the door handle, but I'm aware you have other options. Nevertheless, that, as I say, is the real terror of visitation for me – being press-ganged into sainthood.

It's how I live my life, I suppose. I want to be near you, but I don't actually want to catch your eye. I'm a last-three-pews Catholic. I don't want to be organising the Harvest Festival. I put money on the plate, but I don't even want to be the guy who takes the plate around. I'm not building churches in Africa and, what's worse, I don't know what I'd do if you told me I should be. That Damascus road was quite a busy thoroughfare. If that was your regular spot, you must have seen lots of saint-potential passing by. Were there others? Did some, having heard your sacred commands, just get back on their horse and ride away? How many more, down the years, have done the same, still do the same? For all those stories of inspired individuals responding to your call, what about the ones who sighed and shook their head? I feel for those refuseniks. They must carry that refusal till the end. To refuse the mission is surely to reset the sat-nav for Hell. It could be someone I know. They wouldn't tell. Atheists would think them insane and the faithful would be afraid of the curse they carry, lest it be somehow contagious.

I pray for the chosen, the accepters and refusers. This is the kind of work I feel suited for, petitioning you on behalf of the heroes and the deserters, my eyes to the floor, last-three-pews. Maybe that's why I can't climb out of the pit in that dream. Because I don't really want to. I'm afraid of that final helping hand, afraid of being raised up too high, too close. And maybe afraid that the man with the bad teeth isn't you after all. And why am I suddenly calling it 'the pit'?

ST AUGUSTINE SAID, 'Make me pure. But not yet.'
That's what salvation's all about: timing.

LET'S TALK ABOUT what I saw in TK Maxx today. I need to discuss. I know you were there, obviously. I especially felt your presence near the scented candles. I'm sorry if that seems like stereotyping. Anyway, let me just tell it. They were selling – amid the mountains of ankle-sock multi-packs and not-quite-right sportswear – four different types of buddha. There were some that were just heads and some full-body cross-legged buddhas. Some of the heads had been painted gold, giving them a C-3PO-back-from-his-yoga-retreat feel. There was a sort of off-duty buddha, reclining on one elbow, no doubt getting the blood flowing in his legs again after a marathon bout of full-lotus meditation. There was even a laughing buddha. I'm not talking other-worldly smile. I'm talking full-on guru-guffaw. He was quite a bit chubbier than his colleagues. It seems that particular Eastern religion still cherishes the jolly fat man motif that political correctness has forced off the agenda in the West. As soon as we swapped 'fat' for 'obese' the comedy drained away. Anyway, the laughing buddha was cracking up despite seemingly having sold slightly less well than his fellows. They were all gathered on adjacent shelving in a corner of the store. What I'm saying is that TK Maxx has a buddha section. It sells bargain buddhas.

I don't know how many Buddhists shop at TK Maxx. Many of the stricter ones will be put off by the fly-swatters that are also for sale. I understand that the kindly mystic felt that all life was sacred and some of his more devout followers are prepared to hop and skip erratically in order to avoid stepping on insects. Not easy when you're wearing flip-flops made from dried cabbage leaves. Not for them the smouldering she-goats or pan-fried heifers that your followers were asked to offer up. That isn't a criticism, by the way. Maybe you were on the Atkins.

I'm digressing. My point is, I have massive respect for both Buddhism and its attendant statuary, but I suspect that most of the people buying these buddhas are not practising Buddhists. I think they're buying into a general mystical vibe, a sort of other-worldly equivalent of mood-lighting. So why didn't I see a single Jesus for sale? I'm not here to lecture you about marketing, but it worries me that we've lost so much ground with the I'm-up-for-a-little-bit-of-spirituality crowd. I fear our imagery is a bit too spiky. Let me explain.

Some of these buddhas will no doubt end up in people's back gardens in order to create a bower-of-peace feel. When they think of Jesus in a garden, he's either sweating blood or replacing the severed ear of a hired abductor. It's not very Chelsea Flower Show, is it?

I know our biggest seller is the crucifix and, of course, it's been a Christian symbol for two thousand years. It is an enormous inspiration to me, personally, and I have, more than once, wept as I've knelt before it. I just wonder if it's a symbol with something of a specialist appeal? Has an interior designer ever suggested a room needed something torture-themed? I know a crucifix is no mere decoration, but if we could come up with a mass-produced Jesus image that was more user-friendly – something that, like those buddhas, appealed to people outside of the Faith – we'd have a foot in the door and maybe a tiny seed in their consciousnesses. I absolutely appreciate that your house-call on humanity to save our filth-smeared souls is a story that will always be wrapped around the cross, but it isn't the *whole* story. You must have reclined. It is impossible to be fully human and never recline. I believe you reclined on St John's belly at the Last Supper, for example. But that's probably a bit too homoerotic for the alcoves of Middle England.

Of course, I see statues of you standing, arms spread in welcome, in church every Sunday morning. I recall one in which you looked like you'd just washed your hands and were now searching desperately for a towel, but generally they work pretty well. I still think they appeal more, though, to the converted than the yet-to-be-ensnared. Maybe 'ensnared' is the wrong word. I still think we need to get you down on the ground. Those smart-casual buddhas have the effect that a squatting adult has on a child. They seem to operate at our level while retaining their natural capacity to ascend. I think I've seen a statue of you sitting, but I'm pretty sure you were enthroned, which doesn't really solve the informality problem. The truth is, given that you couldn't even remain horizontal on a lake, we don't tend to picture you reclining but, in thirty-three *terra firma* years, you must have lounged, lolled, sprawled and even spread-eagled. It's a nice thought. It takes the edge off your omnipotence, like a politician in an open-necked shirt.

I would love a Laughing Jesus statue in my living room. I like to imagine the first drafts of the New Testament were packed with one-liners and pratfalls, but the early church went a bit Woody Allen and decided jokes undermined its intellectual integrity and general longing for gravitas. I wonder how many souls have gone unsaved because of that particular editing decision. I've seen fan-art of Laughing Jesus, but it always looks as though the artist has one eye on the canvas and the other one looking for thunderbolts. It makes me really sad that laughter is on the naughty step right next to sex and eating Haribos less than an hour before Communion.

Those giggling, resting buddhas put religion on a bean-bag. They say, 'I'm more like you than you think'.

Those heads show buddha to be a man who isn't too busy to spend time on his hair. People like that. It hammers home his humanity. I love a crucifix in a private chamber, but maybe we need a chill-out Jesus in the front window. Softly, softly, catchee agnostic. That's what I say.

I THOUGHT TONIGHT I'd just listen for a change. No pressure.

I TOLD YOU about my friend's dad dying. Any sign of him? I'll tell you why I ask. I saw her yesterday. She was talking about her wedding next summer. She said she knew her dad would be looking down with a big smile on his face. She asked if I agreed. I said something non-committal and a shadow passed across her. She sought comfort and I was loath to deliver. I don't know, of course, but I just don't imagine the saved being asked if they'd like a window seat. I felt bad afterwards. Still, at least I didn't say, 'Or up with a big grimace'.

The whole question about what happens to the dead, and when, is a source of much confusion for me. Let's take the Heaven-bound, for example. Do they close their eyes, as the beeping machines finally cease beeping, and then immediately open them in Paradise? If so, I don't really understand what happens on Judgement Day. I've always understood it to be the day when everyone receives their afterlife allocations and your great post-temporal apartheid comes into being. I assume the dead will, at your beckoning, come clambering up through the soil. I guess they'll be in a spiritual form too wispy to imagine. Maybe they'll get back some temporary, non-decayed physicality, just for the big day. It's so hard to regiment dust. Will the Risen have shoulders? Either way, they'll find themselves something-to-shoulder with the living, the latter being those who were getting on with their usual stuff when a fiery chariot appeared in the sky and the universal receiving of exam-results suddenly swung into action. But this time it's not anxious schoolgirls craning their necks to see the noticeboard. It's the red-blooded, utterly terrified legions of Earth's last recruits and the fluorescent smears of the dead, also terrified, waiting to find out their Forever. Will it be perpetual bliss or perpetual Gas Mark 5? You know, I'm really glad I didn't go into all this with my wedding-friend.

PERHAPS IF I believed better, I'd have a lot less to say about belief.

JESUS. I WAS reading Matthew's Gospel. Once again, I paused at that bit when you thank the Father for hiding religion's great truths from the intelligentsia while happily revealing them to children. It's so fabulously counter-intuitive. I know St Paul questioned the clear-vision of children – he thought they saw as through a glass, darkly – but Paul, hero that he was, was too angry, too grown-up, for kindergarten wisdom. He was the New Testament's Norman Mailer. Your words made me think about that moment in Mass when the children are taken into an ante-room by smiling middle-aged women so that they can hear a simpler version of the gospel and respond via the medium of wax-crayon. Given what you say about their level of understanding, it is the adults who should be led to the door while the children remain to just believe, on their own terms and through their own sweet filters. Meanwhile, mum and dad sit together in the boiled-cabbage backstage of the church, trying to iron the creases out of their faith, to squeeze past the pragmatism, social pressures and intellectual embarrassment of being a grown-up believer in the twenty-first century. But they're just grown-ups. You haven't actually hidden the truth from them. They're just struggling through the thorn-patch. As for the intelligentsia, or as you call them in the King James Version, 'the wise and prudent', they are so hostile to your truth I imagine them proudly saying to their friends, 'Sorry. I can't do Sunday a.m. I'm busy very deliberately not going to church'.

This could be paranoia, but when I'm part of the glowing ensemble easing out of church after Mass, I often see someone walking in the opposite direction, staring at us with the same facial expression you see on people who cross the road while others stand waiting for the green man to appear. That look that says, 'I don't run with the herd'. I wonder if there's a special map for atheists, with highlighted church locations and Mass times, so they can enjoy as many of these contemptuous passer-by encounters as possible. I wish I could orchestrate that little gang of exiting believers to point an aggressive finger at that passer-by, like leering football fans, and chant, 'Going down, going down, going down'. Those embarrassed by their poor singing voices could instead contribute a menacing undercurrent by simulating the sound of burning – you know, crackling, spitting and the like. Christianity with attitude, that's the way forward.

Anyway, I very much like the idea that the officially designated 'wise and prudent' simply don't get it. I imagine there's a near-impenetrable ego-curtain between them and revelation. They simply couldn't cope with the humility overload. I find this a great consolation. It has long bothered me that atheists sit, metaphorically, on a leather Chesterfield in an oak-panelled exclusive club, sharing highbrow insights with George Bernard Shaw and Philip Pullman, while I find myself in Spudulike with Cliff Richard. I feel better about this exclusive club/fast-food-outlet situation when I consider that the real truths of the universe are more likely to emanate from Cliff than they are from the two literary giants. Like I said, fabulously counter-intuitive. Not that Cliff is a child, of course, but I'm pretty sure you were, in that Matthew quote, referring to the unsophisticated in general. In the King James Version, you say: 'Thou hast hid these things from the wise and prudent, and hast revealed them unto babes'. You know I love that William Wordsworth image of birth: a change of state rather than a beginning. He says, 'Trailing clouds of glory do we come / From God, who is our home'. That glorious simplicity soon gets tarnished by a need to be in control, to feel that it's our hands on the steering wheel. Actually, come to think of it, Wordsworth was a genius, but he got the big message, albeit filtered through a bit of 'green to the very door' nature worship. I guess great poets often retain quite a few wisps of glorious cloud. I'm very happy to have Wordsworth sitting at the table with Cliff and me. Come to think of it, T. S. Eliot can grab a chair as well. He was one of ours. Someone handed me a leaflet once. It had a diagram showing the high, sheer-faced mountaintop where Truth resides. The mountain had meandering paths climbing its heights, paths made by science, philosophy and other great human endeavours. But all these ascending paths went as far as the edge of a scary ravine. The actual peak could only be reached by travelling across a bridge marked 'FAITH'. At the other end of the bridge, the sun shone and the air was clear.

What made me particularly happy about this was that the person who drew the diagram – judging by the quality, a religious enthusiast rather than a professional illustrator – had made the bridge of faith a rickety structure indeed. It made me feel proud that a person religious enough to provide a diagram for an evangelical leaflet to be handed out in the street had portrayed faith as, yes, ultimately leading to eternal truth, but also something that you could easily put your foot right through. If, for example, the science path had culminated in a bridge, it would have been a monumental structure with various plaques that celebrated the designers, engineers and anyone else who'd raised a protractor during the long, complicated process.

In the spirit of that self-effacing artist who drew the rickety bridge, I must admit that I feel the planks creak somewhat when I consider how many of the twenty-first century's top thinkers utterly dismiss the possibility that Christianity is a bridge to anything other than acrylic clothing. I know you said the Father is deliberately keeping the truth from them, but I'm not sure why. I suppose if they believe that human beings are clever enough to reach the truth by combining great knowledge with great endeavour, they're ultimately eliminating the middle-man or, in this case, the middle Son-of-man. I can see why that might feel like a snub. Then again, they show limitless faith in the capacities of mankind. The Father must be flattered by that. Down here, we tend to forgive people almost anything if they're nice about our children.

What happened to all those super-smart believers of yesteryear? Eliot and Wordsworth trod the rickety bridge and – admittedly with some resulting structural damage – so did Samuel Johnson. Then there was Emily Dickinson, Gerard Manley Hopkins and loads and loads of other smart cookies. It just seems that the last sixty years have seen the 'clevers' happily camped on the mountainside, confident that their own bridge will arrive some time soon. Their clouds of glory seemed to get nullified round about the time of the epidural. The Father's hiding-skills have got way too good. I have great respect for Cliff Richard, but I can't imagine him producing a latter-day *Paradise Lost*. I'm glad the babe-like un-sophisticates are still prepared to face the perils of extreme ricketiness, but it would be nice to have a few more clevers in Heaven. Could you perhaps have a word with the Father about the hiding thing? They say you can tell when a civilisation is crumbling because they start burning books. Burning the people who write books is probably quite a bad sign as well.

ONE OF THE things I most respect you for is your post-Enlightenment decision to allow yourself to become unfashionable. It could have just been a sulk, but I like to view it as a creative decision on your part. I believe you came to see going-out-of-style as a form of circular evolution: a return to the source. Let science, drugs and the sexual revolution put on their sell-out main auditorium spectaculars. You're happy with your enthusiastic devotees in the Studio Theatre. We can hear the boom of the showstoppers coming through the wall from next door, but it only makes us feel closer, to you and to each other.

Is THIS A private line or are others listening? I tend to think it's just you guys, the Trinity, and me. And I imagine you keep the conversation pretty much to yourselves. It may be that you discuss it as a group. I say 'discuss', but I imagine it's a sort of cosmic sharing of consciousnesses that you three lapse into without even thinking about it. But do others listen in to me talking to you and, indeed, to the wordless but highly significant hum I occasionally sense by way of a reply? When I say 'others' I'm thinking maybe Elijah, the Virgin Mary, my dead parents, St Boniface, Pope John Paul II and perhaps even the Devil. Does it come through as a sort of PA announcement in Heaven with some auditory overspill also reaching the sulphurous realm? Should it matter to me if it does? It's not as if I'm likely to say anything I wouldn't want Simon of Cyrene to hear. It's just that I come from a Roman Catholic tradition where praying to Mary and the saints is absolutely the norm, so I have to assume that they're somehow in the loop. Should I bear that in mind when I kneel? Is it like when there's a public panel to discuss the next James Bond film and the microphone goes to an audience member and they say, 'This is a question for Daniel Craig' before they ask the question? The other people on the panel get that it's not their moment, but they're still privy to Craig's question and often chip in on the answer. Should I start each prayer in a similar way: 'This next prayer is for God the Father' for example. I've been thinking, again, about which aspect of the Trinity I'm addressing in each specific prayer. Holy Spirit, I almost never speak to you one-to-one. I'm sorry about that, but you're so enigmatic, even by the usual Holy Trinity standards. I'm already grasping for the barely graspable, but you seem to operate on a whole other level of mysteriousness. Rightly or wrongly, I think of the Father and the Son as men with beards. I think of you more in terms of atmospheric pressure. Maybe, if I am seeking something more humanoid, I should follow my Roman Catholic tradition and speak with the saints or with Mary. They'd be less distanced by divinity and also, I suspect, less busy. Okay, one imagines the Blessed Virgin is metaphorically rushed off her feet, but someone like, let's say, St John Boste might be the sort of counsellor who's likely to have a slot free if you needed to talk to someone last minute.

This may all sound somewhat facetious, but I don't mean it to be. Every Mass I attend I declare, publicly, that 'I believe in the Communion of Saints', but how often do I actually have any communion with them? I very rarely, in my private prayer, speak even to Mary and she is basically Mrs God. Am I missing out on a richer prayer-life? I asked about who is listening in at your end because I'd feel easier about talking to St John Boste if I knew one of the Trinity were also on the line, operating like a chat room moderator. Is it possible for one individual saint, slightly forgotten in the suburbs of Heaven, to go rogue and start feeding the kneelers fake news from above? How would we know? It seems much less likely that one of the Trinity could go off-message, what with you three living in each other's pockets the way you do. One reason I worry about praying to Mary and the saints is that if it's wrong, it's probably very, very wrong. It's like I might be moving into golden calf territory, so, consequently, I play safe and stick with the Big Three. But, when we finally get the Grand Explanation, if I find out the whole Communion of Saints thing was indeed bona fide, I'll feel I missed out on something that was probably really deep, challenging and weird-in-a-good-way. Weird-in-a-good-way is one of my favourite religious categories. I like my religion to feel like poetry rather than prose, preferably written in behemoth blood. I don't like it cosy. Jesus may indeed want me for a sunbeam, but I'm hoping he'll then use that sunbeam to melt vampires. I suppose I've always been a bit jealous of the pagans in that their religion seems to be about moonlit glades and water sprites. For me, paganism smells of soil and celandines whereas Christianity smells of Harpic. Of course, the other man's Mass is always greener. But my Father's house has many mansions. The god of the river, the god of the great oak and, of course, the *goddess* of almost anything, has an exciting otherness, but praying to Mary and the saints would give me a kind of legitimate version of that. Mary was born with some sort of magical super-purity; she was visited, out of the blue, by a genuine angel; she had an intense bio-mystical liaison with the Holy Spirit, gave birth to a man-god who would rescue humankind from the eternal void and was then taken into Heaven without any of the usual preliminaries, including, most notably, death. Why are so many people more interested in Beyoncé? The saints, meanwhile, turned sticks into snakes, saw flaming crucifixes amid the antlers of mighty stags, levitated, raised the dead, inherited Christ's wounds and developed an anti-ageing regime that continued to keep them smooth and youthful after numerous years in the casket. Some of these things might, I suppose, fall into the category of myth, but, to be fair, I'm not a hundred per cent sure about the wood sprites. On a less theatrical level, most of the Catholic saints got the title by doing dangerous missionary work, founding churches, getting brutally murdered by non-Christians or just by being very kind. There's something for everyone. If an encounter with the Communion of Saints moved me somehow to the other place, that place where I find myself breathing differently and hearing what sounds like a very distant silence, that place where I can get down to the all-important business of remarkable contact, that feeling of a reachable hand in the dark – can that be bad?

As I wrote down that last bit about the other place and the remarkable contact, I felt it was way too long and I'd have to go back and cut out some massive chunks of text. Turns out it was, in word-count terms, decidedly brief. Strange. Still, I'm back now.

That jolt has reminded me that I'm still addressing you, Holy Spirit. I opened the channel to explain why I rarely spoke to you directly, but I didn't close it afterwards. That's all good. You are, after all, the wind beneath my wings, my divine electricity, I should probably talk to you more. To me, you feel the most interior of the three. Perhaps too close for words. On that note, I wish I hadn't been so throwaway with my reference to yours and Mary's bio-mystical liaison. I didn't mean to talk it down. It's arguably the most important thing that ever happened in the history of humankind. Just saying. Anyway, where was I? Ah, yes. Whenever I attend a public panel, like the James Bond event I mentioned earlier, I make a special effort to address my question directly to the panel-member who's getting the least attention. When I grasp the microphone and say, 'This is for Barbara Broccoli', I feel I'm posing the question in a spirit of human compassion as much as a spirit of enquiry. I'm trying to be inclusive. Whoever the Barbara Broccoli is that day, they glow in their special moment and try really hard to be worthy of the unexpected attention. I wonder if St John Boste could be my Barbara Broccoli in Paradise: genuinely pleased to hear from me and keen to be of service. I respect the global expanse of the Trinity, but it might be a nice change to experience something a little more boutique. SJB would be my man on the ground. When I say 'ground' I mean that springy, white, largely cloud-based flooring you have in the great above. He could be the classic example of a friend in high places.

It could be that I'm doing SJB a major disservice. He might have millions of people requesting his intercession, but my guess is it's a bit less than that. If I could enter into this process with commitment, it could really be something to have regular chats with SJB, one of the English martyrs. It would be like when I hear Mozart's music and think this is direct contact with a man from the eighteenth century, without the filters of language or historical context. It cuts through all that and gets to the core of human communication, unhampered by the grave, soul to soul.

Maybe I'm trying to run before I can walk. Private prayer to Mary would probably provide less of a jolt than going straight to the saints. I already pray to her on a weekly basis in Mass. And she has some great prayers. One of my favourite bits in any prayer ever is that one in the 'Hail, holy queen' that goes: 'to thee do we cry, poor banished children of Eve: to thee do we send up our sighs'. It's less a prayer, more a distress signal. I suppose prayers might look like that from the heavenly vantage point, like a flare rising up from a dark and distant ocean, a brief sparkle of communication.

Perhaps the Blessed Mother's biggest hit is the Hail Mary. There's that bit that says, 'Pray for us sinners, now and at the hour of our death'. I like the idea that wherever or whenever death comes, she'll be there for me. She must get the equivalent of mortality alerts. Then there's the Rosary. I've prayed that on my own floorboards, many a time in the past. I love the use of jingling beads and the way the repeated Hail Marys fuse into a mantra, a backdrop of word-sounds to meditate in front of. It's got plenty of Trinity in it as well, so there's an element of insurance. I want to find out what the fruit is like at the end of the branch, but I'd still like to have one hand on the tree-trunk, just in case.

When it comes to Mary and the saints, I think the big idea is not that we pray *to* them but that we pray *via* them. They are Base Camp One on the way to your oft-dizzying peak. I suppose the theory is that having someone who can pray for us with their saintly hyper-prayer gives us a better chance of reaching the grand destination. If it is wrong, at least it comes from a we-are-not-worthy instinct that it's hard not to have some sympathy with.

Well, thanks for listening. As is often the case, I feel guided through this prayer, a gentle grip on the upper arm leading me to the helpful places. I think I'll go back to the Rosary. I hanker for paraphernalia. But I'll definitely stick with these freeform chats as well. I can run the two alongside each other. The Rosary is a tighter structure, so I guess that will operate like a supporting rhythm, while these prayers are like the improvised solo: some bum notes but some exhilarating discoveries. I suppose it might seem odd that I pray to you about prayer, but refining the transmitter–receiver relationship is important to me and who else do I ask? I don't really have any earthbound friends I can turn to to discuss the technical stuff, the jazz scales and alternative tunings of a vibrant prayer-life. I sense there's a style out there that would fit me perfectly. I'll keep reaching.

ONE OF THE joys of prayer is that you get all my references. I could do a joke about El Greco or Efrem Zimbalist Jr, but there'll never be any need for footnotes. It's beautiful. You're the audience I've always dreamt of.

JESUS. THERE'S A passage in Luke which has been on my mind. It's that bit when you conduct an impromptu prayer-workshop, offering advice and examples for the would-be kneeler. Obviously, if one is looking for praying tips, you're a pretty good starting point, and this is your complete pray-in-a-day guide to upward communication. What worries me is that, quite early on, you warn against trying to impress God by a prayer-technique you describe, quite bluntly, as 'much speaking'. As with all difficult passages in the Bible – those that cause me to severely question my own behaviour – I'm assuming this is something that shouldn't be taken too literally. I hate to think of myself, mid-prayer, remembering yet another thing I wanted to run by you while you subtly turn your arm to eye the holy wristwatch.

Anyway, your how-to-pray jewel-in-the-crown is obviously the Lord's Prayer. This is the grand prayer-template you offer us. And it's not merely a serving suggestion. You are totally prescriptive. 'After this manner therefore pray ye', you say and then you're straight into 'Our Father etc'.

All this suggests I'm already doing it wrong, in that I'm addressing you instead of the Father. This, as you know, is a bugbear of mine, but one could say you give the answer loud and clear: pray like this: 'Our Father ...' Are you honestly telling us not to pray to you? I guess, if the instruction catered specifically for your earthly audience at that particular time, there was no point in praying to you because you were right there next to them. Also, I wonder if there might not be an element of passing the prayoral buck in this. When someone asks me, directly, about doing a charity gig or opening a fete or something, I always tell them to speak to my agent. It gets me off the hook. I like the idea that, when you returned to Heaven, the Father said, 'Did you tell them about prayer?' and you said, 'Yes. I told them to call you'. I imagine there was a resulting loud creak, like an oak tree splitting, as the Almighty's eyebrows were raised, followed by a hurricane-like sigh.

I have to say, at this point, something about your prayer of prayers. 'Our Father' is a great way to start. As openers go it's right up there with 'Once upon a time', 'I woke up this morning' and 'Hello, I'm Johnny Cash'. The 'our' is a masterstroke. I don't know how many drafts you went through with this prayer – I imagine you working on it, writing in the dust with your finger whenever you had a spare moment – but the decision to use 'our' instead of 'my' was a key moment. Even when I pray it in a locked room I feel like I'm part of a communal voice. Once you say 'our Father' you make everyone else your brother or your sister. It's a great reminder that we're 'all God's chillun', as the old song says. If we could just hold that thought, the deep philosophical sigh people give when resolving to calmly put up with shabby behaviour from a family member could also be applied to every person on the planet. It's a sigh that makes allowance, a sigh of tolerance. The first word of the prayer invites us to view humankind as our family, not necessarily deserving of clemency but, rather, having it bequeathed to them through the medium of that universal, forgiving sigh. Yes, I know Cain killed Abel, Jacob gained his brother's inheritance via identity theft, and Joseph's brothers put him in a hole for being a garishly dressed psychic. I'm not suggesting that seeing all humankind as our family would make for an atmosphere of universal harmony. As with our regular family members, we'd still have licence to be exasperated by them, to feel that they don't deserve our affection or to regard them as imbeciles, but that undercurrent of something resembling love – that thing that facilitates the forgiving sigh – would still be there. It might feel like it's buried under forty fathoms of excrement at times, but it would be there. So the prayer starts by putting us all in the same boat, like your terrified fishermen in the storm. Confronted by each other's incompetent weakness, but knowing that the figure striding across the surface of the water can rescue us all.

In the Roman Catholic Mass, we recite the Nicene Creed every week: you know, that prayer where we list all the basic tenets of the Catholic faith: 'We believe in one God', etc. I think you guys are supposed to find the prayer reassuring. We all need an occasional reaffirmation of support. To me, it feels like our manifesto, the Church gathered together, on a Sunday morning, to say what we believe, what makes us different from people who don't believe that and why we're not still in bed. Nowadays there's been a shift and we proclaim 'I believe', the community reduced to an individual, like when you zoom in on Google Earth. It's lonely in this version of the Nicene Creed. It's also scary. When I'm talking truth to power – when I'm saying the big things in a prayer – I like to have a few other sinners at my shoulder, if only as some sort of a human shield. With the Our Father, there's an element of round robin. It's hard to spot the ringleader.

Of course, one could argue that the community evoked by the use of 'our' is, strictly speaking, only those people who say the Our Father, and I may be pushing it to include all the atheists and people of non-Christian religions, but that's just the kind of guy I am and I hope you'll bear in mind my big-hearted, inclusive good nature come the Great Reckoning. Then again, if room in the lifeboats is at a premium on that make-or-break day,

I also hope that, while remembering my big-hearted, inclusive good nature you won't feel any obligation to join in with it. I certainly wouldn't think any less of you for making regular Sunday Mass attendance something of a Golden Ticket.

Addressing the premium prayer to the Father is interesting for me, on a personal level. Since I became a father myself, I have a bit more sympathy for the Almighty. I know you are the Son but, as these two opening words show, I am a son also. Maybe, considering the complications of you being 'one with the Father' and that you were there from the beginning – not common chronology in father–son relationships – your sonship is somewhat more metaphorical than mine. I am a son and my earthly cohabitants are also daughters and sons. What an endless source of pain, disappointment and gut-twisting worry the earthly branch of the family must be. I'm not including you in this. Your sonship has been exemplary. You, probably more than anyone else in the history of history, can safely be described as a chip off the old block. Let's face it, I know it's a claim that lots of older siblings make, but you actually *are* God. We very much aren't. Any prayer I make directly to God the Father – and I'm pretty sure this goes for most of my earthly brothers and sisters too – should, in truth, consist of nothing but an ear-splitting howl of remorse. So this book would have only been available in audio format and would have been quite a difficult listen. My dad used to get upset because he felt my brothers, my sister and I didn't spend enough time together. How would he have felt if we, like the all-encompassing family of humanity, were raping, enslaving and annihilating each other? Human behaviour must be a constant source of disappointment to the Father. I completely sympathise with the flood-reflex.

There is a school of thought, however, that says, in exchange for all this ingratitude, irresponsibility and sneering indifference, what we consistently get back is love and forgiveness. A lot of people don't understand how I, in the light of so much contradictory evidence, could possibly believe in God. What I don't understand is how he, in the light of even more contradictory evidence, could possibly believe in me. Having said that, I think becoming a father has helped me see things a little differently. Once you lock in to the parental love thing, the offspring has to go a surprisingly long way down Evil Road before they can even begin to stem the unconditional flow of empathy and forgiveness.

Parenting, though, can only work properly if you have some form of deterrent to call on when children's behaviour gets out of hand. I'm not saying, Jesus, that I'd actually reach for the pillar-of-salt button if I had one, but, then again, my boy is still only eight. There's so much frustration and disappointment still to come. There will need to be, not poundings, but certainly groundings. It's good to remember that 'our Father', like any other caring parent, is warm and sunny with occasional electrical storms. Bask in the love, but bear in mind that it's a love that's part of a cocktail that also includes brimstone and fire. And that it's a love that can ultimately be lost for ever.

Sorry to go on about this. I know you didn't have children – you were married to the mission – and people going on about parenting can be desperately dull for the childless listener. Don't worry, I'm not going to get the photos out.

MY LAST PRAYER has been nagging at me. You may recall that I celebrated the beauties of the 'our' in Our Father. I felt the topic brought out the best in me. Cometh the 'our', cometh the man. But then I got to thinking about the next phrase in the Lord's Prayer: 'who art in Heaven'. I suppose it could just be there by way of verification. We're addressing our Father who resides in Heaven rather than the one who resides in Wolverhampton with his new girlfriend, Beverley, who we despise and who wears an ankle-bracelet despite being in her early fifties. I know that doesn't describe *every* earthly father but I just offer it up as a for instance. The point is, this part of the prayer does seem to suggest a certain pulling of rank. We're talking about the Father with a capital 'F', not some biological enabler. It's an unnerving theme that runs through scripture: choosing between, or at least, placing in order of importance, God and your family. I guess the Father asking Abraham to kill his only son is one of the more graphic examples. The knife was raised. Abraham was all set for son-slaying when the angel stepped in with a last-minute reprieve. Do I admire Abraham for his religious conviction in this episode? If I do then I think I also have to admire suicide-bombers for theirs. It's all about homicide as a way of proving true belief, a sort of inverted martyrdom.

I love the Old Testament – I read it every day – but, as a selling-document, it could do with a solicitous edit. Or, at least, some dazzlingly inventive footnotes. When I'm arguing with atheists about my beliefs, I'm always really hoping they won't mention Abraham preparing to barbecue his only son. I keep mentioning the 'only son' thing, but only because that fact gets hammered home in Genesis. I'm not suggesting that if Abraham had a load of kids (which he eventually did) it would have lessened the horror of his apparent willingness to cut and carbonise one of them. You can't justify child-murder on the grounds of there being 'plenty more where that came from'. As it turns out, no atheist has ever challenged me on the Abraham–Isaac episode. That's the great thing about arguing with them; they've rarely done the groundwork.

I'm lapsing into light-heartedness, but the fact is the Abraham–Isaac story hurts me every time I read it. The Father asks Abe to sacrifice his child and there's no backchat, no protestations or pleading: just cut to Abraham and son heading for the altar. It gets worse when we realise Isaac is helpfully carrying the wood for his own incineration. And then there's another gut-wrenching detail when the boy says something like, 'Hey, guess what! We forgot to bring a lamb for the sacrifice'. I'm sorry, but it's just horrible. The old man poised, knife in hand, over his unsuspecting child. When the angel calls a halt, I get the horrible feeling we're supposed to feel happy. But it wasn't, as it turns out, even the case that Isaac was a necessary part of some mystical ritual that we could never understand. No, it was merely a con, a grim leg-pull. The angel doesn't actually say, 'Just kidding', but it seems to be inferred. At this point in the narrative I really need one of those aforementioned dazzlingly clever footnotes to convince me that the surface narrative – an apparently cruel God reveals himself to also be a needy prankster – is, in fact, merely the vehicle for some great truth. I want to be convinced that my ignorance of Hebraic sacrifice-ritual small print, an uneven scriptural translation and a general mists-of-time communication breakdown has accidentally turned a celebration of deep faith into a Japanese secret-camera TV show.

Why, why, why? Does the story actually operate as an example of perfect obedience to God? Would the Father want that kind of obedience? You, Jesus, know him better than anyone. Just a few chapters earlier, Abraham is haggling with the Father in order to save the lives of a bunch of licentious strangers in Sodom and Gomorrah. Now, when asked to kill his own son, he suddenly becomes an unquestioning yes-man.

I see no proof of faith here. Abraham is more likely motivated by fear. What separates the haggling and the unquestioning is Sodom and Gomorrah being utterly destroyed. Arguing with post-fireballs-from-the-sky-God probably takes more courage than even Abe could muster. Of course, there's always the possibility – my own favourite interpretation – that Abraham never had any intention of going through with the execution. That he'd learned, in his previous dealings with the Father, that a bit of guile from the snivelling earthbound is often appreciated. Anyone who plans to be the father of a nation better have a wide selection of crafty manoeuvres up his sleeve. Abraham looked like he was all set to do the deed, but we'll never know what would have happened if the referee hadn't stopped the fight.

I realise I may be applying a whole set of strictly human considerations to this incident, which could be dispersed like a handful of dust by the mighty winds of unfathomable cosmic logic. What does one act of filicide matter in the context of eternity? I don't know. But, by way of an argument, I could quote the Father's 'Thou shalt not kill' and your own statement that if anyone harms a child they'd be better off in the sea with a millstone around their neck.

I don't like to get forensic, like this. Partly because I'm scared to challenge you and partly because I know the Bible, certainly the Old Testament, is a scrapbook of myths, proverbs and truths that need not necessarily also be facts. Maybe 'I know' is slightly overstating it, but that's my humble-to-the-point-of-kneeling opinion. I've also read, somewhere, that the Abraham–Isaac story is a foreshadowing of your own death; you know, the sacrifice of the son motif. I'm sorry, but it doesn't quite work for me. As far as your own journey is concerned, it always feels, even as the cross is raised, that you have your hands on the steering wheel, whereas Isaac is bound, gagged and waiting in the boot.

Anyway, about that God versus family thing. I'm thinking of that time when you were a kid and you went missing and left Mary and Joseph frantically searching for you. I know that knotted feeling in the stomach when you lose sight of your kid for ten seconds. You were missing for three days. And then, in the temple, when they finally find you – and I can imagine how those three days went for them – you say the equivalent of 'What's all the fuss about? You should've known I'd be in my Father's house'. That put the 'f' in Joseph's fatherhood very much into lower case.

Then there's that time … Look, I sound like I'm nagging, but if the priest is going to read these stories to us, week in, week out, you can hardly blame me for remembering and referring to them. I think that was always the intention: take away these stories and apply them to your everyday life, employ them in your everyday conversations. Anyway, I'm thinking about that time when your mum and relatives turn up to one of your gigs and can't get in, and when you're told about it you say something like, 'Who is my mother and family? Anyone who lives a holy life is my mother and family'. I know I spoke to you before about the joy of seeing everyone as family, but if my mum had been waiting outside my house at the time, I'd have let her in first and then carried on with my Family of Man pontificating. I enjoy sharing my great wisdom more than most, but, as Dean Martin once sang, 'Show me a man who loves his mother and I'll show you a man who's man enough for me'.

Please don't take all this as a reprimand. I just think we earthlings struggle to come to terms with the cold, hard priorities of the big picture because our own pictures are so small and domestic. On one level, I find it strangely reassuring when you say wince-inducing things in the New Testament. It makes me think that the compilers had such respect for your words that they didn't dare tamper with them, even when those same words make you sound a bit spiky and thus make their evangelising a much harder sell. That suggests that we're getting the real deal, without trims or embellishments. It gets us really close. I can almost smell the nard.

ARE MY SPOKEN prayers diluted by writing them down? A laptop is a cold intermediary. Is the incense spread ever thinner by my desperate grabbing at it? It's okay. It seems only right that you should get the live versions, with all their raw immediacy. They reach you before they've even left me: soul to Saviour. I can share the transcripts with my fellow travellers. Hopefully, they'll acknowledge and accept the shortfall.

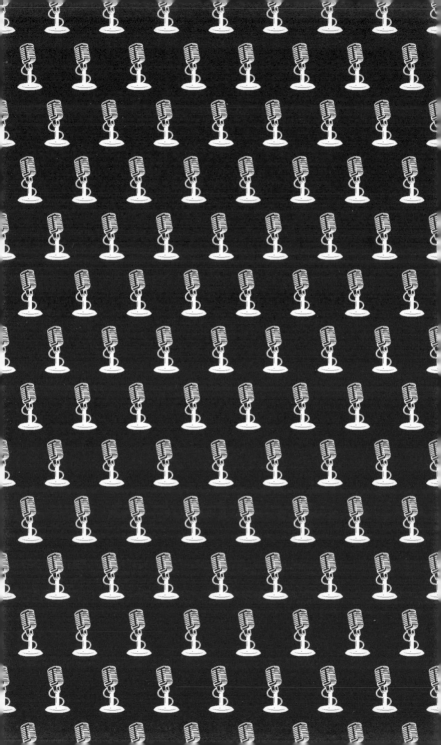